Self-Publishing
Write a Great Novel, Book 4

by
G. R. Sixbury

Self-Publishing: Writing Fiction for Readers

(Write a Great Novel 4)

Copyright © 2017 by G. R. Sixbury

Published by Kansix Books, Inc.

ISBN-13: 978-1-947317-04-8

ISBN-10: 1-947317-04-0

Dedication

Thanks to all of my students. Hopefully I managed to teach you as much as you taught me.

Preface

I grew up in the traditional publishing world. I sold my first (and subsequent) short stories to major editors. I sought and found an agent and was fortunate enough to sell novel-length work using her services. Back in those days, self-publishing didn't really exist. You couldn't just log on to a web site somewhere, upload a cover and some content, and order a proof copy. That idea wasn't even a glimmer in someone's eye.

What we did have were vanity presses. They're still around and work pretty much the same way they always did. Using a vanity press basically means you pay a company to take your typewritten manuscript and turn it into a published book. Vanity presses, which are also called subsidy presses (they are the same beast with a different name), often claim that they will help you sell your book after it's finished, but this isn't true. They've made their money. They certainly aren't going to help you market your published book, which is a much more difficult and uncertain task than just getting a manuscript into print.

Unlike those days of yesteryear, self-publishing today isn't about seeing your name in print on the cover of a single book. If that's all you want, feel free to consider a vanity press. It'll be a lot less work, and since your goal isn't to make money, there's nothing wrong with paying someone to produce a vanity publication that you can gift to your friends and leave to your grandkids.

This book is about succeeding as a self-published author. Put another way, this book is about succeeding as a small press publisher, because as a self-published author who's trying to make money, that's what you are.

Table of Contents

Part I: Writer As Publisher

Stigma, Schmigma

For most of history, self-published meant lousy. That's because if you wrote a quality book that people wanted to read, traditional publishers would buy it. Eventually. If you kept sending it out year after year and if you kept writing new, high quality material . If traditional publishers didn't buy it, good reasons often existed why that book never saw print.

There were exceptions. A few excellent books were self-published. For those books, publishers weren't interested because the audience for the book was too small. Or the publishers thought the audience was too small. Credit the worst of the self-published books from those days for creating the stigma against self-published books that was common and expected until just recently.

Before looking at the (mostly) glorious revolution in publishing, let's be clear. Traditional publishing has never been perfect. If professional editors never made mistakes in their quest for bestsellers, they wouldn't have rejected Agatha Christie for the first five years of her writing career. A dozen of them certainly wouldn't have rejected J.K. Rowling. Between these two women, they've sold an estimated three **billion** dollars in novels. Without a doubt, forcing new writers to storm the castle that is traditional publishing in a vain attempt to see their book in print killed off the writing careers for most the writers who tried. For the majority of those writers, these were mercy killings. But a great many wonderful writers were felled in the massacre along with the schleps. Overall, I believe the system still worked. Until about forty years ago.

A Bit of History

Traditional publishing suffered a major blow in the late 70's even though they didn't recognize it at the time. With the invention of the personal computer, suddenly anybody could write a book. As one of the last dinosaurs who wrote, edited, and polished his first novel longhand before creating a mistake-free typewritten copy, I can tell you that the amount of work and frustration called for by such a tedious process weeded out a great many people before they got started. What this meant is that finished novel manuscripts weren't streaming into the publishing houses in smothering numbers, at least not compared to later. With a bit of help from assistants, editors and agents could keep up. Once personal computers and word processing programs became common, the deluge quickly grew out of control. Form rejection letters became common. More assistants were needed. But with television stealing readers and publishing costs on the rise, less money was available.

So many factors contributed to the problems facing traditional publishing at the end of the twentieth century that it's impossible to blame any one factor. I could write a book on this subject alone. To be brief, as distribution companies became larger and regionalized and their buying agents became nationalized, pockets of readers were ignored. At the same time, living on an editorial assistant's salary in New York became excessively painful for anyone who didn't have another source of wealth or income. That mostly limited the pool of editorial assistants to a select group of youngsters with a particular financial, educational, and geographical background that bore little resemblance to readers in the rest of the country. Out in the real world, readers became increasingly frustrated by the ever smaller selection of fiction from writers who they wanted to read. As a result, they quit reading completely or restricted their book buying to known commodities. The best-known authors got more money per advance, sold more novels than ever before, and represented more and more of each company's bottom line. As the publishing houses slotted less money for new writers or established writers with steady but unspectacular sales, patience for these writers grew short. Readers who liked these writers were out of luck. Selection and quality suffered. Publishing companies failed and were gobbled up by larger companies. Quality and selection suffered further.

While forcing writers to be accepted by major publishing houses kept the number of new authors down, it did little to improve the entertainment value of the novels that were published. I'm not trying to be critical. Editors are people, too. They have likes and dislikes. Unfortunately, with such a small group of people whose opinions mattered, it's inevitable that their likes and dislikes didn't always match up with the reading public at large. Certainly the quality of writing (the prose) was better under the traditional model—some self-published novels these days read as if they were written by an illiterate six-year-old—but shock of shocks to most traditional editors, normal readers don't seem to care nearly as much about prose as they care about story and characters (and price).

Which brings us to the publishing world of the early twenty-first century. While I have no doubt that most of the New York publishing industry would disagree with me, I would contend that the success of self-publishing was preordained the moment a distribution method became available for self-published novels because the needs of readers were not being met by the traditional model.

Enter Amazon, CreateSpace (and others). While a ton of books that (in my opinion) should never see the light of day are being published in record numbers, the flip side is that those same books are available to people who do appreciate them. Instead of our selection being controlled by a handful of publishing professionals who decide what everyone likes to read, suddenly the marketplace can decide for itself.

Welcome to the twenty-first century.

And Now for Something Completely Different

As of mid-2016, the world of publishing was well on its way through a major upheaval. If data from Amazon is examined, what we see are years of falling market share for the big traditional publishing houses and huge growth in market share from independently published (read self-published) books. The small presses, which of necessity have always been more sensitive to their readers, have a market share that seems to be holding steady or even climbing. As to why we should pay attention to numbers from Amazon over numbers from other sources, that's because *85%* of all non-traditionally published U.S. book sales *in any format* happen on Amazon.com.

Numbers that are perhaps more important turn up when we examine authors who are making their living from writing (earning $25,000+/year) and who are just getting started (meaning their first book debuted three or less years ago). If we examine those writers, most of them published their own books. To clarify this further, there are more than twice as many new authors making their living publishing independently as there are authors being published by the big, traditional houses, by small and medium sized presses, and by Amazon itself… combined! If you're a new author making his living, chances are better than 2 to 1 you're publishing your own work. While numbers like this never remain static—your should feel free to track down the latest and greatest information on the subject—I'm betting that any changes that have occurred since I looked at these numbers are in favor of the self-published authors. Perhaps the odds are up to 3 to 1 now that you'll be self-published.

Anyone who criticizes self-published novels as being no-good or low quality or not worth their consideration should be pitied. They might be right, but it's a bit like a carriage maker screaming at passing automobiles. Readers have spoken clearly with their hard-earned dollars. Most of them don't seem to care whether you're published by

New York, by Alma, Arkansas, by Amazon, or by your own good judgment.

If you write it (and publish it), they will come, dollars in hand.

What, Me Worry?

In simplest terms, if you feel like you can handle the demands of publishing your own hard work, there is no reason at this time not to do so. If anyone criticizes your finished work that's selling like crazy, you can pat them on the head and thank them for their opinion. And then write and publish another book while they're still waiting to hear back from their publisher or their agent.

You're the Boss

One of the great things about being the boss is not having to answer to anyone else. One of the worst things about being the boss is not being able to blame anyone else when things go wrong. Confidence is one of the best attributes any writer (or any boss) can have. As a publisher of your own work, what you're looking for is a healthy dose of what I call critical confidence. For me, embodying critical confidence means periodically and methodically examining everything you're doing for validity and effectiveness, then charging ahead to the best of your ability.

To be an effective boss, you need data. Once you have that data, you should be decisive, committed, and confident. You must also motivate your employees. For self-published writers, this means motivating yourself.

Becoming a great boss isn't easy or trivial, but many of the skills can be learned.

Do you have the skills and the desire to be self-published? Under what circumstances should you self-publish rather than seeking a traditional publisher?

Pros and Cons of Self-Publishing

You bought this book, so obviously you're interested in self-publishing. Why read about the pros and cons of your decision? The choice is already made, right?

Not necessarily.

Unless you've already published your own work, you probably haven't encountered much of what you need to know to be successful. Even if you're a perfect candidate for self-publication, you can use this section as validation for your decision. Better yet, use it when you're helping your writer friends decide on the best publishing model for their work.

Below I've broken out the advantages and disadvantages of self-publishing. Use the list below to determine whether your best course of action is to try to publish your novel through the traditional model or whether you would be better served publishing your book yourself.

Advantages

- Better royalties, typically earning twice as much on printed novels and nearly three times as much on electronic
- Complete control over what you publish, how you write it, what cover it has, how you market it, when it's released, how long it stays on the market, etc.
- Guarantee what you write will be published if you believe it's good enough to be published (a huge motivator)
- Ability to publish books that would otherwise be unpublishable because of limited expected audience or controversial content

Disadvantages

- Responsibility for all parts of the publishing process, requiring competence, initiative, and effort in many areas beyond writing

- High level of productivity required for best results
- No professional approval required, allowing you to publish some embarrassingly awful books
- Typically minimal or non-existent presence in physical bookstores as well as school and public libraries
- Less visibility on electronic book sites than what is enjoyed by traditionally published work
- No guaranteed pay
- Full liability for anything you put in print

Analysis

For me, the greatest advantage self-publishing provides is that it's a guarantee of publication. This sounds trivial, but knowing your work will be published when you finish it gives you an incentive to finish the work that you just can't obtain when any doubt lingers about whether you're wasting your time.

Why Not Both?

A common sense approach would suggest trying to publish your novel the traditional route first. If and only if that fails, self-publish the novel. In my opinion, that's not the way to go. For one thing, it will take you years to determine your novel's not likely to see print via the traditional route. Think how many novels you could have self-published in the meantime. To be clear, I'm not saying that if you go the traditional route and fail you shouldn't consider self-publishing your work. I'm saying that failing shouldn't be part of your Plan A.

Most writers can be divided into two groups. Those who should self-publish and those who should try to for publication via the traditional route. What's the difference? I've given you the pros and cons, but it's not that simple. Publishing, whether traditional or self, is a minefield, but not just any minefield. The giant stone of time is rolling down the hill of ever-diminishing energy, and it's ready to ready to squash you flat if you stop to consider any path too long. I know tons of writers who say such inane things as, "You need to take your time writing a novel because your brain needs time to process the infinite possibilities your imagination can create." Baloney. That's like saying the only way to tear down a house is to wait until it falls down on its own. Sure, it's a heck of a lot less work, but if you're willing to pick up a sledge hammer and start pounding away, you can reach your goal a lot more quickly.

Making everything more complicated is the sheer mountain of self-doubt that's more than willing to convince you that you can't do what it takes to make your career as a writer a reality.

Why not just try both? The same reason you don't drive from one town to another by just heading in roughly the right direction and guessing which way to go at every fork in the road. Sure, that path might be more interesting and might allow you to discover parts of the country you wouldn't see otherwise, but that way takes an amazing amount of time and your time is limited much more than you think.

Does It Even Matter?

The answer regarding which publishing route is best for you starts with what you need from your writing. If all you're looking for is an interesting hobby where you might write for forty years and have nothing published beyond a handful of short stories and a novel or two, choose whatever path seems the most comfortable to you. If you're not willing to trade a good chunk of your life to see your work in print, don't. Meander along whatever path allows you to be the most productive, because when you're a non-productive writer, being more productive is really all that matters. You can't publish if you don't write.

Tons of writers only have incentive to write if they're writing what they want to write without regard to the market. If you're one of these writers, it also doesn't matter which route you take. Your chances of success in that case will be a combination of dumb luck, skill, and talent. You can be wildly successful under either publishing model. If you happen to enjoy writing the type of novels everybody wants to read, you're going to do well. If you write novels nobody wants to read (regardless of how well they're written), you're going to struggle. You might as well struggle under whatever model gives you the most incentive to write.

So the choice of which model to pursue only matters if you're productive and you're willing to write to market to some degree. If that's the case, there's still a difference, but seeing it is difficult, because it's all shades of gray. To help you make the right choice, we need to dig deeper.

Writer for Hire

Many successful writers will tell you that you should only write what you want to write. While it's true you need passion for what you're writing, absolutes like this aren't particularly useful. If you like writing novels about grizzly bears, whether you write about a grizzly bear set in Montana or a grizzly bear set in Wyoming may not matter that much to you, but it might make a huge difference in how that novel sells. If you follow the write whatever you want edict, you won't consider the market when choosing your bear's home state. Some writers have a mental block against exactly this type of market consideration. Some editors do, too, which may explain why the novels they buy don't sell that well. The folks in this elitist artistic camp are welcome to their opinions, but if they did any market research, they'd discover you can't predict what type of original novel readers will like, but you can determine what readers are buying now. If I tell you there's a current need for military mysteries where the main protagonist is a wounded veteran, could you write a novel fitting those requirements? If you don't think you could, pick another dozen specific examples in genres you like better and ask yourself the same question. If the answer is always no, I'd recommend you stick with the traditional publishing model, because you're a high-risk publisher. Sure, you might be successful, but I wouldn't want to invest in your publishing company. And when you're a self-published writer, that's exactly what you are: You're a one-person publishing company.

The difference between you and the typical publishing company is that you have a stable limited to exactly one writer. While most publishing houses have the luxury of considering thousands of novels and publishing only the ones that fit their marketing model, you're publishing every single novel this dreck writer (meaning you) puts out. Don't get me wrong. I'm not insulting your writing skills, but if your self-publishing company puts out ten novels that don't sell, you're not going to have the highest opinion of this lone writer, either. It's a numbers game. If you only have one shot at success (meaning one writer, you), don't you want that shot to be the best it can be?

If you're serious about your writing success, the decision as to whether to go the self-publishing route or go the traditional route comes down to one determining factor. Are you willing to listen to the market? Can you do the research to determine what novels are likely to sell and then set about producing novels that have the best chance of success you can give them? If not, stick with the traditional publishing model. If you're writing the greatest novels the twenty-first century will ever see, chances are good you'll be "discovered", published, and wildly successful. Granted, even after publication on the traditional route, you'll still need to write to market to have the best chance at keeping that success going. Don't believe me? Talk to a few best-selling authors who are so disgustingly sick of their own series that it takes all of their will power to finish the next book. If they hate it that much, why do it? Because it pays the bills. Whether you go the traditional route or the self-publishing route, if you're successful, you're going to have huge incentives at some point to write what you don't feel like writing. Why? Because you're relying on it to sell and sell well.

Step 1: Decide What to Write

Perhaps you're thinking, hold it! I already have my novel finished, how can this be Step 1? If so, you're probably right: This isn't the first self-publishing step for the novel you just finished. But it should be the first self-publishing step for every book you write from here on out. Before writing a single word, decide what type of novel (you can write) that is likely to sell the best and write that one.

Publisher As Writer

If you were Chief Editor and CEO of the largest publishing house in the world, you would have total control of which novels your company published. So which novels would you choose to publish? Would you simply pick the ones you liked best? Possibly. But what if I could wave my magic wand and guarantee that you'd like all of them exactly the same. Now which novels do you choose? Stick the titles of the novels on the wall and throw darts at them? Consult a fortune teller? Weigh the manuscripts and pick the heaviest one?

You might cry foul at this point and claim there's no way you could like all of them exactly the same, but in a self-publishing company, that's the case. As a writer who self-publishes her work, each novel you finish is the same. You're going to publish it. That decision is made, so the amount you like each of those novels never comes into play. If the quality of or preference for the novels never comes into play but you're still trying to be as successful as possible, there's only one logical way to decide which novel to publish: You choose the novel that you think will sell the best given the current market.

The main difference between my make-believe, wand-filled scenario and what you actually experience as a self-published author is that you make the decision on which novel to publish before you've written the novel.

Writing to Market Is Writing to Sell

I can already hear the dissenters screaming from the back of the room: "You can't write to market!" And if you're talking about the traditional publishing world, that's reasonably good advice. The only write-to-market exceptions in the traditional world are established authors writing more of the same stuff they've been selling, which they've already shown has good market value and which they alone can write (because, hey, it's their stuff). That's not what these dissenters are talking about (and not what I'm talking about either). We're talking about writing a similar-feeling novel to one that's currently all the rage.

If a novel comes out featuring a talking grizzly bear who's actually an alien from planet Spandex and it sells like mad, the tried and true advice is that you (as a new writer) can't take advantage of the sudden demand for novels featuring talking animals that are really aliens. This is true, but what no one likes to admit is that this kind of piggy-backing happens constantly in the entertainment world and has for far longer than anyone can remember.

Think it's coincidence that Rob Roy and Braveheart both came out in the same year (1995)? Just how many big-budget movies based on historical Scottish folk heroes do you suppose come out each year? Think it's just chance that True Blood came out one year and The Vampire Diaries was released the next? Even going way back and overseas, you have the bizarre example of *Mr. Peabody and the Mermaid* and *Miranda*, both British comedic mermaid pictures released within months of each other. I mean, come on. *Mermaids!?* What are the odds?

These are films, you claim. With novels, it's different. I would agree, but only because traditionally published novels take so long to produce. It's still not unusual for a manuscript to take a year or more after it's finished to appear on the shelf of your local bookstore. It's hard to write to market when the market has changed three times before your first attempt comes out.

This can't be stressed enough. In the old days, if you identified a new, popular type of novel, you would be right in thinking that readers likely would be wanting more novels similar to that one. You and every other writer. And quite a few of those other writers would have been a lot more well-known that you were. And when you finished your talking-animal-that's-really-an-alien story and sent it to an editor, guess who was going to be sick of reading that type of novel? Precisely. The very editor who you hoped would buy your novel. He already had fourteen similar novels under contract with some of those other writers. The last thing he wanted was another talking animal book.

"Why can't authors create something original?" he would cry out in frustration. Okay, maybe not literally. But this is the source of the information all those dissenters are relying on. Simply put, it's outdated.

That's because we all have computers (Kindles/smartphones/e-readers). In the old days, readers who wanted a book similar to the talking-animal-who's-really-an-alien one they just read went to the science-fiction section and quickly discovered nothing similar at all. Now those same readers can go online and quickly track down every available novel that features a talking animal who's really an alien. Voila! Seven (or seventy) similar novels to choose from. Of course they'll buy at least one. Maybe even yours.

Readers have always enjoyed buying new novels that were somewhat similar to ones they've enjoyed before. The difference is that our modern world provides readers with the tools they need to find those similar novels with ease. And it provides you, the writer—or I should say, the publisher—with the tools to discover which types of novels are selling well. Those are the ones you want to publish.

How to Choose

Note that I said that readers want more of the similar, not the same. Readers aren't looking for an exact rehash of a favorite novel. They're looking for something that has a similar feel. They're hoping to find a new novel that they enjoy as much as the last novel they read from their favorite author. If you examine the proclivity of many readers as a group, you'll discover that their tastes fall into recognizable patterns. A great many different recognizable patterns, but patterns all the same. Some people call these tropes. Others call them genres. Some folks combine tropes and genres to make some kind of a literary Cartesian coordinate system. I will stick with the terms genre and subgenre.

The genres that come to my mind first are romance, suspense, mystery, thriller, fantasy, science fiction, religious, horror, western, and action. From there, the subgenres are too numerous to mention. If we pick one at random, such as mystery, we might end up with subgenres below it like crime, serial killer, heist, kidnapping, murder, noir, organized crime, and vigilante justice.

Why are genres important? Because it's often how a reader finds your novel (or how that novel gets recommended to him). If you just finished a novel that could be classified as a serial killer, mystery novel, you might like another serial killer mystery novel. How does this help you, the writer? It allows you to choose a very specific genre that's not so inundated by novels that a new novel will almost certainly get lost in the shuffle while also letting you choose a genre that has the number of potential readers you're looking for.

For example, Amazon sells a lot of romance novels. A LOT. Does that mean you should write a romance novel? No. What it means is that if you were already interested (and passionate about) writing a romance novel, you should consider tweaking that romance novel so that it fits in a desirable subgenre of romance, a subgenre where authors exist who are selling novels similar to what you were already thinking about writing.

There's a great deal of numerical voodoo you can do to determine exactly what genre you should target. I don't provide details here because the precise method that works now probably won't work in the future. What's important is the general methodology, which would have worked in the past as well as today.

That methodology is simply to find novels from new authors that are selling well that are a type of novel you would be willing and able to write. Preferably you would restrict your search to first novels from new writers. The reasoning is that new writers have no following and no existing readers, which means their new novel sold on its own merits. Granted, it could be that they've written the novel of the century and captured magic in a bottle. Contrary to the thinking of those in the writing-is-artistical-magic crowd, that's the exception rather than the rule. Most new novels that are successful are good novels that fit into a genre that a significant number of readers like. Granted, the novel should be as good as you can make it to have any chance, but this is true regardless of type or publishing model.

Series, Seriously

If you can write a series of novels rather than a stand-alone novel, your chance of being read and making a living at your writing are considerably higher than if you do stand-alone novels. Why is this? Are series novels better?

No. Series are more profitable over time than equal quality stand-alone novels because it's simple math.

Let's look at the situation where you've written four novels: the first two novels in your *Money Is Good* series and two stand-alone novels called Written First and Written Second. (Granted, we should probably fire our title creator, but it's easier to follow this way.) You release *Money Is Good, Volume 1* and *Written First* at the same time. For this example, I'll allow *Written First* to be a better novel than the first book in your series (best case scenario in support of stand-alones). The readers respond and *Written First* makes more money. But what happens when you release the next two novels? When *Money Is Good, Volume 2* is released, you not only sell copies of this novel but you also sell copies of Volume 1. Plus, when sales for the second novel in your series starts to slow, you can run discount specials on the first volume in your series to get readers to try it, which provides sales for the second novel in your series that you couldn't have realized any other way. When you release *Written Second*, you get few (if any) additional sales for either your series or *Written First*.

What this means is that each subsequent novel you release in a series makes money for itself and money for every novel in the series up to that point. When you release a stand-alone novel it makes money for itself. That's it. Granted, a few readers will notice who wrote the novel they just read and go looking for other novels they've written, but practical sales numbers show this is way less common than most writers believe (and way less common than common sense would suggest).

Provided you keep the quality of the novels in your series above a minimum threshold set by your readers, this multiplying sales effect is compounded for each subsequent novel released in your series. By the time you're up to seven or eight novels in the series, your stand-alone novels don't have a chance.

Does this mean you should never write stand-alone novels? Not at all. But if you want your publishing company to start out life as a success, releasing only series novels in the beginning ups your chances considerably.

You Still Matter

So I've recommended the type of novel you should write. Find a type that sells and write that as the first in a many book series. But don't forget to consider your own abilities and tastes. If you attempt to write a novel you don't want to write, in that way madness lies. And much frustration. Not to mention failure.

Yes, you want to write to market, but you want to write something that's close to what you would have written anyway. Just as the best lies are based on truth, the best novels you can produce are based on your own tastes, feelings, talents, and inclinations. Trust your instincts. Especially when those instincts tell you to write a novel that fits the market.

Step 2: Keep Your Output High

The most important advice I can give any writer is to write. Write as much and as often as you can. Of the two hard and fast rules I have, the first is to write. This is never more important than when you're the sole writer in your own publishing company. Let's face it, the number of authors in your stable of writers is pathetic. You can't be successful if you have no product to sell. But it goes beyond that.

Did You Write Something?

We live in a Attention Deficit Disorder society. We binge-watch entire series of television shows. Technology changes faster than pioneer settlers changed their underwear. If you take years to produce your next novel, your entire career is going to start over with the release of each new novel.

On the other hand, if you produce several novels a year, momentum builds with the release of each novel. You get more recommendations from the online search engines, you make more money because you release more novels, you get more readers because you have more chances to gain those readers, and you take giant steps toward being a professional writer instead of a wannabe writer. More important, you develop the reputation among readers as a writer who can be counted on to deliver new material, which makes you worth following and worth reading.

Sure, it's always possible your first novel might be wildly successful. If it's that good, people will wait for your second. But why make them? Unless you're one of those sparkly vampires in real life, your days are numbered. Sure, you can fool yourself into thinking that rewriting your novel fifty times will make it better than writing it just once. You may even be right, but for most writers it's not true. A novel that's been rehashed fifty times will read like it's been rehashed fifty times.

Unless you're already writing *5,000 Words Per Hour*, you can improve the speed at which you write. Do this and you will write better, write faster, and finish more books. For one way to do this, consider picking up my first book in the Write a Great Novel series (*Writing Quickly While Writing Well*).

Don't Rewrite

Novels aren't like wine. They don't automatically get better with time. Two difficulties exist in knowing how much you need to rewrite: 1) You can't trust your own judgment, and 2) You can't trust anyone else's judgment, either. All you can do is to write it as well as you can, get it edited **once** by someone who seems to know what she's doing, and move on.

This don't-rewrite advice is scorned by a large segment of the professional writing community, and with good reason. There are some truly awful self-published novels coming out these days. They contain more grammar mistakes than a failed English test. But they're out there and available for purchase. That novel you're writing and rewriting and polishing isn't. What's more, that incompetent writer just put out another five novels while you were agonizing over whether you had the almost right word or the right word.

Don't get me wrong. Writing well is important. What's hard for most writers to accept is that getting their prose just right only impresses a tiny number of readers (many of whom are other writers). But here's the thing. Writers don't buy as many books as avid readers. And the readers, for the most part, don't care. They read for stories and characters, not prose.

So, wise and powerful Oz, are you saying I should publish my first draft? Absolutely not. Especially when you're just starting out. Write the novel to the best of your ability. After a brief cool-off period to give yourself some objective distance, rework the novel, polish the resulting manuscript, and then get that finished novel edited, line-edited, and copy edited by professionals who are trained to do so. Yes, that means you'll be paying them, so choose your editors well.

The key with self-publishing is that you're not looking for perfection. You're looking for good. With traditional publishing, you didn't have a choice. You couldn't risk having an editor fail to read (and purchase) your novel because it had a punctuation mistake in your opening paragraph.

Step 3: Pay for What You Need

Finishing your book gets you a good share of the way down the road toward self-publication, but you're far from finished. In addition to creating a professional manuscript, you'll also want to have the following set up before you release the first title from your new publishing company:

- Have your book edited and copy edited
- Generate a professional cover that looks great full-size and as a thumbnail
- Format your book for publication in e-book format (and if desired, as a printed novel)
- Produce a marketing plan and marketing materials
- Create and publish a web site

The first question you need to answer regarding these items is whether you'll do them yourself or whether you'll contract others to do them. On the side of doing these yourself, you'll pay less, you'll have full control over the outcome, and you need to come up with the key information for each regardless who does them. On the negative side, you're unlikely to do as good a job on any of these as an expert would, all of them will take time away from your writing, and you have a greater chance of doing something really stupid.

For me, the greatest determining factor in whether you do these is money. If you simply can't come up with the money to pay someone to do these tasks, you don't have much choice. But if you have the money, I urge you to consider farming out as many of these as possible. Even at small publishing houses with a single editor on staff, the editor typically doesn't create the covers, the web site, or format the book. If you want to run your own publishing house, even with you being the only author, it's a good idea to pay attention to what other professionals in your line of work are doing.

Editing and Copy Editing

I mentioned in the last section that you should have your novel edited, line edited, and copy edited. This is good advice for your first two to three novels. Unless you already have these skills at a professional level, it's likely you'd benefit from some professional advice. The problem is finding good professional advice. Before you begin looking, you first need to know what you're looking for.

Developmental Editor

A developmental editor (sometimes called a content editor) is who most of the population imagines when they conjure up a mental image of an editor. These are the folks who recommend changes to your novel. At this point, you're looking for all the advice you can get, whether it be with story, characters, motivations, pacing, or use of language. Having said that, you shouldn't be hiring a developmental editor to fix your novel. *You* should fix your own novel before you send the novel to the editor. What you're looking for from the editor is to improve what you already have and catch any mistakes you might have made. Plus it's a second opinion from someone who knows nothing about the novel other than what's on the page. This fresh set of eyes can be invaluable.

Having said that, you (and you alone) know what's best for your novel. Don't allow a developmental editor to move your novel in a direction that you never intended. To be a good writer, you must know what type of novel you're trying to write and what you're trying to achieve in each scene and in each chapter. If you get advice from an editor that doesn't make sense within that framework, you must ignore the advice, no matter how good that advice might seem on the surface.

That doesn't mean you ignore your editor. You should have taken care to find the right editor before hiring them, so consider what they've said carefully before you reject it.

If this sounds complicated, it's because it is. One of the hardest skills a new writer can learn is when to ignore advice and when to follow it. I'd love to give you some handy rule that would allow you to know if someone's advice is good or bad. All I can say is that you should try to hire editors who are writers themselves and who've written a novel you can read and respect.

After getting input from your editors, you'll likely be rewriting sections of the novel, which is just one more reason not to spend the extra time swinging for the fence of perfect prose before the edit. Few things are harder for a writer than throwing out several pages that took hours and hours to get "just right." But there's a huge difference between perfect and good. Your prose should be as grammatically correct and as strong as you can make it in a first pass. Don't sweat every word, but don't blunder your way along. You want your editor to be concentrating on your story and characters, not the hundreds of grammar mistakes and plethora of typos.

Line Editor

Only after you've received feedback from your developmental editor and altered the novel in response to that feedback should you hire a line editor. Line editors do what their title implies: They go through your manuscript line by line and attempt to improve the language. Their goal is not to change what you've said but to help you say it better. They compress prose, improve verbs, correct language usage, and improve dialogue. A good line editor is worth their weight in gold, but many line editors perform their function by rote. They remove all your adverbs and most of your adjectives, all references to time, and all uses of the verb "to be." When you're starting out, it's useful to employ a line editor to get a sense of how your writing can be improved, but if you agree with the style a line editor creates, you can learn to clean up and improve your prose just as easily as most line editors can.

Copy Editor

After you have received some editorial advice and have utilized the changes that made sense, polish the result. Make it as good as you can. Only then should you send it off to a copy editor. Why not let the copy editor find your mistakes? Because writers should have the skills necessary to copy edit their own work. If you don't polish your manuscript and make it the best you can before sending it to the copy editor, you'll never know if you would have caught the errors the copy editor finds. Plus the more mistakes you force your copy editor to fix, the more likely they will miss some of the corrections they should make. It's much easier to spot any given mistake in a clean page of prose than it is to catch the same mistake when it's mixed in with seventy-four others. What you're looking for from a good copy edit is another pair of skilled eyes that can catch your grammar and punctuation mistakes, spelling and diction errors, and inconsistency slip-ups.

Hiring the Right Editors

Take your time finding the right people to edit your manuscript. Good editors are hard to find. For your developmental editor especially, try to find someone who works with the same type of book you've written. Each genre has its own tropes and requirements. A good romance editor might be a lousy science-fiction editor (and vice-versa). Try to get recommendations from other authors and ask questions. Shop and compare. The internet makes all of this far easier than it was before the World Wide Web existed, but the process is far from foolproof. Above all, try to be the best you can be at all of these skills before you seek professional help. A good writer should also have the skills needed to be a good editor, line-editor, and copy editor.

Cover Generation

Unless you're a professional artist with excellent marketing instincts, you'll probably want to hire someone to do your cover. There are plenty of artists who specialize in creating covers for novels. Find several and compare. Good book covers still sell novels. You want your cover to be the best it can be. The problem is that nobody can agree what "good" is. There are only a couple universal truths.

- Your cover should look good as a thumbnail graphic
- Your title and your name should be easy to read

Beyond that, everything's open to debate. Typically your colors shouldn't clash, but sometimes people do that for effect. Browse books that are a similar type to yours. These are the novels your readers are buying. What do those covers look like? Figure out the look you want, then hire someone who can create that look for you.

Formatting

Getting your book into a form that will look great across all e-book readers and will look great in print is a daunting task. There are entire books not to mention author service sites devoted to the subject. For novels, there is an easier way. Google "Kindle Simple Formatting Guide" and "Format for CreateSpace" and follow the guidelines given.

What!? Why would I simply tell you to follow Kindle's and CreateSpace's advice? Because at this point in time, selling on Amazon is the only model that makes sense for a self-publishing operation that's designed to make money and is just starting out. (Kindle is the e-book format of choice for Amazon and CreateSpace is the print format of choice for Amazon.)

But why limit yourself to Amazon? Because even if you combine the sales from every other outlet channel an independent, self-publishing author can access, those sales will pale in comparison to what you can make on Amazon. Instead of wasting your precious resources trying to satisfy all the formats available, charge ahead with Amazon and call it good. Still not convinced? Here are some reasons to go exclusively with Amazon:

- Only one e-book and one print format to worry about
- As of May, 2016, about 85% of all independently published book sales *in any format* in the U.S. happen on Amazon
- If you're productive and you write good novels, Amazon does a lot of your marketing for you
- One source for all of your royalty information, saving time both monitoring sales and gathering sales information for tax purposes

If you decide to market your novel everywhere, there are several author services available that will format your novels. As with any services you hire, do your research and hire quality professionals.

Marketing

The most important marketing concept to embrace as a self-published author is that of brand. Your goal is to have readers recognize your name and buy your novels because of that name. For all your novels, your name should be prominently displayed and easily readable on the cover. The same goes for your series. They should recognize the name of the series and should be able to tell which book in the series a particular novel is from the cover alone.

To increase your series branding, you should use similar covers, the same font, and the same color scheme across all books in the series. (Not the same colors, but the same style. Books that are part of a series should look like they belong together.) This similarity across novel covers provides a professional and recognizable look that readers identify and respect.

To further increase your brand, you should consider hiring a publicist to put together a marketing plan for you. While this isn't necessary, it saves time and allows you to access expertise that would be unavailable otherwise. What's important is that if you self-publish a novel, you need to get the word out. After all, if people never hear of your novel, they can't buy it. Having said that, if you have the time and inclination to do your own marketing, do so. No one's going to care about your novel as much as you do. Even if you hire a publicist, you can't just write them a check and leave them to their own resources. Remember, you're the boss. Act like it.

Web Site

Some authors will claim that you don't need a separate web site these days. You can just use services provided by Facebook, Twitter, and other online social sites. I disagree. Not only do you have full control over your web site, you can also use it to build up your email list of folks who are interested in your books. This email list is invaluable. It represents both a list of your fans and a way to communicate with them. For any author starting out, the most valuable asset you can have is a solid base of fans who like what you write. Let's face it: Most people won't like what you write. That's no reflection on you. Different people have different tastes. What your email list gives you is an unsurpassed way to target marketing on your next novel to a group of people who have liked something you wrote in the past.

There is too much. Let me sum up

Self-publishing is not for everyone, but if you're a normal writer starting out today, self-publishing is your most reliable way to make a living if you're a highly productive writer who produces quality material written to market, and who isn't afraid of a little marketing work.

- Anyone who criticizes self-published novels simply because they are self-published is living in the past; feel free to ignore them.
- Self-published authors earn better royalties, have more control over both content and marketing, and are guaranteed publication.
- Choose your publishing method before you write your novel rather than using self-publishing as a backup plan.
- If you're a non-productive writer, being more productive is all that matters, so choose the publishing method that provides you the most incentive to write.
- As a publisher with only one writer in your stable, writing to market makes good business sense.
- If you're writing novels, series generate more revenue than stand-alone novels of the same quality.
- The single greatest factor that will determine whether you succeed as a self-published author is how fast you can write well.
- If you can afford it, pay experts to edit your manuscript, produce your cover art, format your

manuscript, market your novel, and generate your web site.

Part II: Series

Money, Money, Money

Money equals readers.

Whether you're the most free-spirited, giving person the world has ever known or the most materialistically greedy grinch since Ebenezer Scrooge, being a successful writer still comes down to money. Even if you give away everything you write, your popularity will be less than it would if people paid for your work. This is because a lot of people make money off writers: Publishers, film and TV producers, toy makers, fast food chains, clothing manufacturers, poster printers, marketers, and many more. These folks aren't going to promote a series of books that doesn't make them money.

In general, the more money you make as a writer, the more readers you have for the books you produce. This isn't always true, but desiring to make money from your writing is not as selfish as it appears to be. You want to give your readers a chance to enjoy your stories, don't you? The very nature of fiction is entertainment, which provides amusement and joy to people the world over. That's a pretty noble purpose when you think about it, regardless how much money you make doing it.

For the average writer, the most reliable way to make money is by writing a series. That's why I've dedicated part of this book to the subject. Whether you love series or hate them, they remain the most reliable form of income you can generate.

Why is that so? What makes novels in a series better than stand-alone novels?

In "Step 1: Decide What to Write", I outlined the financial logic behind why series make more money. It boils down to this: Subsequent books in a series help to sell earlier books in the series whereas stand-alone novels don't reliably lead to sales of your other work (no matter how contrary this is to common sense). But it goes beyond that.

At its base, readers have preferences. The type and setting of a novel is a bit like wine regions. If I go into a store looking for a bottle of wine, the easiest way for me to find one I like is to stick with regions I know and like. Readers are no different. It's also a matter of simple practicality.

Imagine you're a film producer. You're looking for a new story idea. You're a series bigot, so you buy only stand-alone novels to turn into movies. The producer down the road only buys the rights to series. Guess what happens. If you are both equally talented, the movie producer down the road becomes rich, famous, and powerful while you make one bad decision and go broke. That's because it's a lot cheaper to raise money in Hollywood for a proven commodity than it is to raise money for a story you believe in.

The same is even more true for television series based on books. If your stand-alone novel was deep enough to drive an entire television series, it was more than deep enough for you to create a great series of novels instead of just one. That's the reason it so rarely happens. Most TV series based on the written word are based on a series of novels rather than just one book. Don't believe me? Check out the most popular series on TV that came from a novel (or from a series of novels) and see which happens most often.

That doesn't mean that stand-alone novels don't have their place. If you want to write only stand-alone novels, feel free to do. You're fighting a bit of an uphill battle, but if your stand-alone novels are ten times better than any series book you'd ever put out, you're making the right choice. If that's the case, skip the rest of this part of the book. On the other hand, if you're like most of us and need to write series in order to pay the bills, the following sections will provide good information on how to do that.

Be a Serial Thinker

One of the reasons I've pushed series so much in this book compared to stand-alone books is because too many series were never meant to be series at all. Unfortunately it's not as easy as many writers think to turn a great stand-alone novel into a great series of novels. Overlap certainly exists—most great characters do just fine whether their lives consist of a single novel or span hundreds of novels—but almost without exception, series are better if they were originally conceived as a series rather than being tacked on after the first novel sold well.

By definition, conceiving a series before writing the first book means you plan your series to some extent before you start writing. While I'm sure there have been many successful authors who didn't plan anything in advance, most good series were created before a single chapter was ever written.

To Grow or Not To Grow

One of the great fallacies in most modern writing circles is that your characters must fundamentally change throughout the course of a novel. I don't believe this. For every series I ever gave up reading, I quit mostly because the main character had changed. I liked the original character. That's why I bought and read books two through eighty-five. But in that eighty-sixth book, I realized that the character who I loved so much had been growing distant for a while now. He just wasn't the same character I fell in love with. It was time to end the relationship.

I'm not saying that your main character shouldn't change at all, but never forget that your readers like your main character. That's one of the reasons they're reading your novels. If you change that character, you risk losing those readers. With a stand-alone novel, this is less important. If the novel was enjoyable and thought-provoking, readers are less likely to harbor any regrets about the changes the hero experiences. But if you write a series of novels where the main character is constantly changing, you're bound to stumble eventually upon a combination your readers don't like. At that point, they quit buying your books. Game over.

When you do allow your main character to grow, your goal is to improve what readers don't like and keep what readers do.

For example, in the Janet Evanovich series featuring Stephanie Plum, one of the biggest reader complaints you see in reviews is that Stephanie remains an inexperienced idiot. She often succeeds through assistance from others or through sheer dumb luck. It's clear a lot of readers believe Stephanie would be a better character if she grew in intelligence and competence from novel to novel. Since she's constantly gaining experience, it violates the laws of common sense for her to remain so inept after several novels have gone by. In comparison, Harry Potter is a much more accomplished wizard by the end of the seventh novel than he was at the beginning of the first. The gradual increase in skill he gains from novel to novel is normal and expected for most characters.

At the opposite end of the spectrum lies the problem of improving your main character too much. For many readers, nothing gets older faster than a character who already had fantastic capabilities in the first novel and rises rapidly until they have godlike capabilities in subsequent novels. Two problems with this exist: 1) You have nowhere left to improve and 2) The character goes beyond someone readers can relate to.

When you create the main characters for your series, either leave them room to improve or don't have them improve much.

Readers don't love your characters for their perfections alone but also for their flaws. For every step you allow your character to move forward, consider having them take a step back in some other area.

A good technique for creating a series character that grows in a way your readers like is to create two versions of your character. The first is your character as he appears in your first novel. The second is your character as he will become by your last novel. While the exhausting ordeal of writing the series may change your original intent, having both versions of your character in mind not only gives you a target at which to aim but also provides an existing version of that character to test for adequacy. You want your character in his final form to be passionate, active, capable, interesting, and believable.

The most frequent problems I see with characters who grow are that they lose their passion, they fail to be interesting (often because they've lost their entire sense of humor), and they're no longer believable because they've become too incredible for credibility.

Your best bet, as you grow your character, is to leave their essential core unchanged. Sure, they've been altered by what's happened to them (your story), but at heart they're the same person your reader first fell in love with.

The easiest way to do this is to give your character a strong set of core values and a ton of depth. While you should always know volumes more about your characters than what ends up in your books, the amount of knowledge you need for a main character from a series is much higher than what you need for the main character from a stand-alone novel. Give them room to grow that doesn't involve changing who they are.

Exception to the Rule

Some series have different characters (even different main characters) in every book. For these novels, it's not the characters that drive the series forward, but the story. For those series, none of these comments related to character growth are relevant. For novels from this kind of series, characters are equivalent to those found in a stand-alone series.

It's All Relative

While your characters don't change in fundamental ways, erelationships between characters are constantly changing. Typically it will be an ebb and flow where the relationships end up back close to where they started, but some progression will inevitably take place. This is particularly true with any romantic connections between your characters. If two characters fall in love, have sex, or even have a fundamental disagreement, their relationship is never quite the same again.

Often relationships between characters are as important to a reader's enjoyment of a series as are the characters themselves. If that trio of characters who became lifelong friends in book one are still around in book seventeen, most readers want their relationship to be intact (although a bit altered). When they triumph over the big bad together, the reader's enjoyment is magnified.

Take Me to your Leader

The main character in a series is the driving force behind that series. Create a lousy main character and your series is doomed before it starts.

You're looking for a character who cares deeply about the people around her and who cares deeply about solving the problems you throw at her. You're going to throw problems at her book after book after book. She needs that depth of passion to keep going when the going gets tough.

She should be a doer, not a complainer. That means a problem solver, preferably a non-conformist problem solver. There are plenty of people who follow the rules. In fiction, we have a name for those people: Boring! You're not looking for someone who breaks the rules for her own gain, but for the good of others. Individuals are more important than groups here. Her friends, her family, her dog, her cat, and her pet hamster are vital to her sense of self. She'll sacrifice a lot for the people who matter, although she'll always be trying to sacrifice herself first. "Kill me instead," is a good mantra for her to follow.

Fortunately she's not going to die as a result. That's because she's capable of great things. She may not seem like it on the surface, but that depth of character you've given her brings her through when others fail. She will excel in some areas and lag in others, but she will use her strengths to conquer the evils of the world. Often, she will not come through unscathed, but she will always come through.

Finally, she will be larger than life. You're looking for someone who has iconic qualities. She needs to be a symbol that others can recognize, identify with, and long to be.

Or you can just make her really funny. Humor conquers all, as Janet Evanovich has proven. That's because humor is interesting. Humor is fun. If your main character is so interesting she's irresistible, you can break any rules and ignore any advice I give you. Most writers aren't capable of creating a character who's that interesting without a little help.

The Big Question

Three main kinds of series exist: 1) Those that have an overall story arc that continues from book to book, 2) those that have major story elements that carry over from book to book, have a significant impact on the plot, and have no end in sight, and 3) those with books that stand alone but have a world (setting) and characters that carry over from novel to novel.

The most famous example of the first kind (building story) is the Harry Potter series. While each novel has its own story with its own conclusion, all novels build to an overall story conclusion. A well known example of the second kind (meandering carryover) is the Harry Bosch series by Michael Connelly. Events that happen to Harry in one novel impact Harry in the next one. The most famous recent example of the third kind (mostly independent novels) is by Dan Brown. The Robert Langdon novels certainly have carryover from novel to novel, but they don't share one building story arc that will be resolved by the last novel in the series.

The first and second kinds of series are by far the most common. Readers like series because they share similar elements. In general, the less elements shared between novels in a series, the less readers enjoy the series. Most readers like the inside jokes and interesting tidbits that are gleaned only for readers who have read previous novels in the series. It's not universal. Some readers want to pick up any book in a series and be able to enjoy it regardless whether they've read any of the other books in the series.

Some authors bore their loyal readers to tears by trying to make this easier through the repetition of facts any reader of the series already knows. For example, each of the subsequent Harry Potter books becomes increasingly painful in the early chapters as readers are tortured by repetition of information we already know. Eventually J. K. Rowling gives this up as a bad job, but only after several novels.

When designing a series, one of the first decisions you should make regards which of the three types of series your series is going to be. If you choose the second or third types where you have limited carryover from novel to novel, you can get away with having a lot less series story arc. If you plan to do the first type of series where you're really telling one long story in multiple installments, the importance of planning and having an overall story plot is increased.

While character depth in a series is important, story depth is equally important. (You can get away with mediocre characters if your story is strong enough.) Since you're writing a series of novels rather than one novel, everything is expanded. The techniques you use to plot a single novel are the same techniques you use to plot a series of novels, except in maxiature. (Yes, I know maxiature isn't a word, but it should be.) You're looking to build the tension and raise the stakes until everything hangs in the balance (and is resolved) in the final book.

Creating a Series Story Arc

The best way to create a story arc that can support a many novel series, in my opinion, is to create as many story threads as you can weave together—and then weave them together. This sounds easier than it is, and it doesn't sound all that easy. What I'm talking about here is an attempt to link everything together into a greater whole.

How do you do this? Patience, determination, talent, and a hell of a lot of work. I know no one wants to hear that, but while your overall story might come to you while riding a train from Manchester to London, it doesn't come alive until you've filled it out with as many threads as you can master.

The only reliable way I know to do this is by figuring out your main story arc and then working backwards from the end.

For example, your hero might need to be the best sharpshooter in the world by the last scene of the last book in the series. Starting with that fact, you spiderweb your way out. Your main character needs an overwhelming reason to become such a good shot. Maybe he had a chance to save his wife from the villain in novel three, but he missed the shot, and he swears that will never happen again. Perhaps he goes broke and in desperation he opens a gun club where he gives shooting lessons. A young arrogant punk embarrasses him in a shooting competition. Rather than trying to get revenge or cause the young kid problems, he has the kid give him shooting lessons. So now we need to give our hero reasons to go broke and to be humble enough that he's willing to take lessons from someone half his age. Maybe he decides to make the young kid a partner in his gun club. Maybe the young kid dies and he decides to seek revenge.

The key is that you start with what you need and grow your story organically. While I prefer to work from end to beginning, some writers do better working from beginning to end. Either way, you mix and match and move possibilities around until you start seeing connections. This is where the talent comes into play. That ability to see the dramatic in the every day is something that can be improved upon but not created from nothing.

It's interesting to note that this tapestry can be weaved by starting with story and allowing it to define the characters, starting with characters and allowing them to define the story, or, what happens most often, starting with both story and characters and allowing them to define each other. You can even start with your world and use the circumstances of the situation to determine the characters and story you need.

Always there must be character motivations that arise from the natural circumstances of the original events. The forces at work should be as powerful as you can make them, and they must oppose each other.

In the most basic and time-honored stories, these forces are good vs. evil. They oppose each other because they can't coexist. Order vs. chaos. Freedom vs. regulation. These types of polar opposites make excellent land masses upon which to build your story civilizations. In most stories, such polar opposites begin in focus. Black vs. white. Right vs. wrong. As the novels progress, the situation grows more complicated. Readers learn the evil side isn't all evil and the good side isn't all good. There are legitimate reasons for both sides, but in the end, if you want to have a series that survives the ages, the easiest way to do it is to make it easy for the reader to root for one side over the other. When the final triumph comes, it's a total triumph rather than a triumph with reservations.

Your World

The process of world-building is like writing: There are nearly as many methods for creating fictional worlds as there are writers who create them. A few common guidelines exist:

- Always know much more about your world than you've told your reader
- Create opposing worldviews
- Don't overcomplicate your world, especially in the first few novels
- Know the history and possibly the future of your world as well as the here and now
- Create opportunities for humor

Often humor comes from characters, but those characters need a world to live in.

For most novels, culture is a vital part of any worldbuilding you do. All cultures have a reason for their existence and reasons why they are the way they are (and your reason can't be "Because I need them for my story"). Cultures aren't uniform. You're looking for beef stew here rather than chicken broth.

Sometimes You Need a Plumber

Understand how infrastructure works. This is more obvious in a magical or science-fiction world, but it's true for real worlds as well. If your main character is a detective who's constantly solving crimes, why is the detective stuck at the same position? Why haven't the higher-ups promoted him to captain or at least lieutenant? Your answer may lie in the traits your character exhibits, such as a complete disregard for authority, but it can also exist in the world itself. Maybe all that matters is seniority rather than performance.

A vital part of worldbuilding is going beyond what you need and understanding what repercussions those needs create.

Learn How to Piss Someone Off

To drive a series forward, you want cultures that have fundamentally different views and beliefs. That means you need to know why those cultures vary so greatly. What factors shaped the cultures and why do the people of those cultures care so much about keeping their culture intact? Allow those differences to have repercussions. After all, if one side got it completely right, why wouldn't every side adopt the same world view? Note that "because they're evil!" is not an acceptable answer to that question.

Keep It Simple Smeagol

The simpler initial view of your world given, the easier it is to create a dramatic story that takes place in that world. Especially in a series where the depth of a world can be explored over the course of many novels. Limiting the world view in the first few novels allows a reader to gain familiarity organically rather than having it thrust upon them.

Don't Forget to Laugh

Because the emotional stakes in a series tend to rise over time, many authors forget how important humor can be to a reader's enjoyment of a novel. For most humans, the more stress they encounter, the greater their need for laughter. The reason humor is difficult to maintain in a series often stems directly from the author. As more storylines weave together in a never-ending crescendo, it's easy for an author to become overwhelmed. Often, the first part of the series to suffer is the humor. Making sure to keep humor in a series not only benefits the reader but often it benefits the writer, too.

There is too much. Let me sum up

If you're a writer for long, you will probably want to write at least one series at some point in your career. Many successful writers spend their entire careers on a single series.

- All else being equal, books in a series will make more money (and be read by more readers) than standalone books that are not part of a series.
- Novels that are designed to be part of a series from the start are typically better than those based on a standalone novel that was turned into a series.
- The main characters in a series are not expected to change as much as many characters do in standalone novels. Changing the main characters in a series too much often results in lost readers.
- The main heroes in a series are often iconic characters who tend to be larger than life.
- To create a great story arc for a series, weave many storylines tightly together.
- To build a great world for your series, create a deep and detailed world with a rich history and future. Don't overcomplicate the world, but have opposing factions that can drive your plots forward.
- Never forget how important humor is to a series. Especially in a series, it's easy for drama to overshadow humor.

Part III: Marketing

Not My Job

I wish someone else had written this book and I had read it before Tor published my first novel. Even though I'd been in the business long enough to know that traditional publishers barely lift a finger to promote a novel by a new author and that most of the marketing was up to me, I didn't know how to market my novel. Even so, I didn't stand on the sideline doing nothing. I managed to snag articles in several newspapers, did four book signings, and one radio interview. I created a web site devoted to the release of the novel. I created marketing materials and distributed them in any place that made any sense at all.

And it meant nothing.

The reason was simple. It just wasn't enough. I didn't understand that marketing my novel required nearly as much effort and time as writing it. More important, doing 90% of the marketing required to sell a novel isn't much different than doing 10%. Until you reach a critical threshold of readers that allows your novel to start selling itself, you really have no chance.

Fortunately, in today's world, marketing is easier than ever before. It still takes times, but using the techniques covered on the following pages, it's possible to effectively market a first novel and make a real impact on sales.

"Wait!" you scream. "That's why I sold my novel to traditional publishers in the first place—so that I wouldn't need to do all this marketing stuff!"

Forgive me while I shake my head and tsk-tsk sadly.

When it comes to marketing, it doesn't matter whether your book is being published by one of the big five out of New York or whether you're publishing it yourself. Unless you received a six-figure advance, the amount of marketing you will receive will do nothing to sell your book. Even if this isn't the case, do you really want to take that chance? You wrote your novel so that people could read it. They can't read it if they don't know it exists.

The good news is that the techniques you use to market your novel are pretty much the same regardless of how the book is published. The main differences relate to what you're allowed to use for your reader magnets (covered in a moment) and the amount of control you exert over your cover and blurb.

If you want to be a successful writer, you better learn to be a successful marketer.

The Fine Print

Many of the techniques I cover are directed at writers who are just starting out. It's easy to market your work when you have a large body of work to market and a loyal following of devoted readers. What I'm more concerned with in this chapter is marketing your first novel or your first couple of novels. Having said that, plenty of the techniques covered here will serve you well throughout your writing career. Adjust my advice as needed to fit your current situation.

Brand I Am

People love brands they can trust. In our modern world, buying decisions are more complicated than ever before. If you can find a brand that delivers, your buying decision becomes easy: Just look for that brand.

For writers, this concept of brand is not limited simply to name alone. Sure, if you're an avid reader who loves Stephen King or Dean Koontz, you buy a novel simply because it's written by one of those writers. But what about J. K. Rowling? She has plenty of brand clout, too, but her personal author brand pales in comparison to the Harry Potter brand. When I talk to people about their favorite novels, I hear plenty of readers who say they love Harry Potter. Few say they love J. K. Rowling. It's not that they don't love J. K. Rowling—they do—but when they think of her, they think of Harry Potter first.

As authors, when we talk about branding, we have two considerations. If you're a writer of stand-alone novels, you're marketing your own name. If you write series, you're marketing both the series name and your own name. After all, you'll probably finish that series someday and you'd love your readers to join you on your next great adventure.

What you want are satisfied readers who trust your brand. Violate that trust and you risk losing that reader forever.

Pseudonyms as Imprints

Most readers like certain kinds (genres) of novels more than others. That's why traditional publishers invented the imprint. Imprints allowed readers to easily distinguish between different types of books. You don't want the fans of your hard-boiled police procedural series making the mistake of picking up the young adult romance novel you just released expecting to find a police procedural. Some writers think this situation is fine—it's another book sold—but sell a book and lose a reader forever is not a good tradeoff.

Under normal circumstances, as a lone author, you have no control over imprints (whether you're self-published or whether you sold your novel through traditional channels). What you do control is the name you put on a book you wrote. That's where pseudonyms come into play. Having pen names for each of the different types of novels you write keeps you from disappointing readers who are expecting Jane Austin and get Jane Casey.

Using pseudonyms to distinguish between novels written in different genres isn't necessary, but it is a time-honored technique used by writers for decades. Research shows that midlist and below writers receive few crossover buys between the various genres they write. While releasing all of your novels under your own name has a certain appeal, it's hard to justify from a marketing standpoint if you write novels in widely differing genres.

The key question in determining whether pseudonyms are appropriate is asking whether most of your current readers would like your new novel. If not, branding that new novel differently with a pseudonym is a no-brainer.

Talk Once, Sell Many Times

I know hundreds of writers who think a great marketing plan consists of doing signings, composing a blog, interacting with people on social media, and otherwise building their readers one at a time. The problem with this concept is that it's not efficient. For every hour you commit to marketing, you have one less hour to write. While every devoted and admiring reader is precious, there is a better way to gain those readers.

The bulk of your marketing time and dollars should focus on doing the marketing once and having the chance at many readers in return. Part of this is getting the word out to places and people who are likely to spread the word further still. Here are a few examples of this work once, get many readers philosophy:

- Television, radio, and newspaper interviews
- Book reviews
- Advertising
- Web Site and author pages
- Newsletter

All of these techniques involve very different skills. As such, we should probably take them one at a time and see what we can make of them.

Television, Radio, and Newspaper Interviews

Entry into any of these outlets is typically an uphill battle. Lots of people have something to sell. What you must have is something to offer as well as something to sell. While successful self-promotion through the media is a topic worthy of a book unto itself (or perhaps a series of books), a few general pieces of advice are handy:

1) Learn how to write a press release. An easy way to do this is to google "how to write a press release." It's a learned skill, which means it's a skill *you* can *learn.*

2) Figure out a way to leverage any knowledge or background material that went into your novel. Likely targets are science, history, and geography. This is one advantage provided by writing about real places rather than made-up towns and cities.

3) Learn how to give a good interview and remember that while your eventual goal is the promotion of your novel, your immediate task with everything you say is to be entertaining.

Don't get discouraged if your first attempts to land an interview fail. Also, no interview is too small, especially when you're starting out. That interview for the local paper gives you valuable practice for later in life when you're being interviewed for an audience of millions. If you don't prepare for it to happen, it never will.

Book Reviews

The person reviewing your book is more important than the review itself. Does that person have a following? If so, what kind of following? You want reviews from people who mainly read novels like the one you wrote. If their focus is narrow, the chance of their review being viewed by others who would want to buy your book goes up. So, if you want the "right" people to review your book, start by looking at who reviewed recently-released books that are similar to yours and send your book to those people for review.

Beyond that, try not to pay too much attention to reviews of your book. Whether a particular reader liked or didn't like your novel is irrelevant. The only helpful information you can gain is why a reader felt the way they did. Were they the wrong type of reader? If so, then their negative (or positive) review says more about them (or more about your advertising and marketing) than it does your work. Learn from your reviews and move on. It's guaranteed people exist who will hate your book no matter how good the book is. If you have no negative reviews, you simply haven't found those people yet.

Only pay attention to positive or negative reviews when the reviewer is kind enough to say what they liked (or didn't like) about your novel. For example, if you introduced a new character in the third book of your series and that character receives mention in multiple reviews, then that information is pure gold. Do the readers like the new character? Do they hate him? Do they like him in general but hate his political views? While you can't bend your series to the opinions of your readers, it's just good business sense to nudge the series toward the likes and away from the dislikes of your readers. Either that, or adjust your marketing so that you're not targeting people who aren't going to like your book no matter how well it's written.

Advertising

It'd be great if I could tell you exactly what you need to do to advertise your novel effectively. Unfortunately, every book is different just as every writer is different. As with reviews, you want to target your advertising toward people who have a good chance to like your novel. Advertising across the board is so ineffective that it's useless.

Opportunities for advertising your novel change almost daily. To decide if an advertising opportunity is right for you, evaluate it on the following criteria:

1) How well does it target the readers you want versus readers in general?
2) How much does it cost per response?
3) How well can you measure your success?

In a perfect world, your advertising will reach only the readers you're interested in reaching, will cost a fraction of what you make per sale, and will provide every useful metric you can imagine. In reality, one or more of these areas will be less than you would prefer, but they provide a useful measuring stick for effectiveness.

Since advertising is so complex, I've covered what you need to know in much more detail under "The World's Oldest Profession" section.

Web Site and Author Pages

Having your own web site is important, because it's the only internet based web site over which you have complete control. Ultimate power has its uses. Plus the cost of having your own web site is minimal for a professional author. If the revenue from your writing doesn't provide enough funds to support your own web site, then you're still in the wanna-be writer, hobby phase of your career. There's nothing wrong with that, but you have to invest in yourself at some point. Creating your own web site is as good a place to start as any.

Many services provide free pages for authors to use for promoting their work. Some common examples are the author page on Amazon, a celebrity Facebook page, and the author page on Goodreads. Many others exist. While it can be time-consuming to get all of these set up with relevant and intriguing information including the image of your smiling mug, the update rate of these pages can be minimal. Some helpful guidelines:

1) All public displays should be as professional and as well thought out as you have time to make them.

2) Update these pages regularly, but don't overwhelm your followers.

Along with web pages spreading the good word, feel free to utilize Twitter and any other electronic communication service that allows you to reach your readers. The warning I give here is that using a service like Twitter for self-promotion alone is like working at a restaurant for 8 hours every day because you're hungry. Sure, you're surrounded by food, but it takes you forever to get anything to eat. Said another way, feel free to use these frequent update services if you're already using them. If not, they're probably not worth the time they'll steal from your writing.

Newsletter

For most authors, your newsletter should be nothing more than a quick chat with your readers to announce something *related to your work* that they would find relevant. You can certainly do more than this, but the length and frequency of your newsletter relates directly to how useful and entertaining your readers find your newsletters to be. I know writers who can hit their readers with a newsletter every day. The readers eat it up because the writer is such a dynamic personality or shares such fascinating information that the readers simply can't get enough. For other writers, each time they send out a newsletter, they risk losing readers. Know your strengths and your weaknesses. Lean on your newsletter accordingly.

Besides deciding what to put in your newsletter and deciding how often to send it, you need to know who to send it to. The answer to this question is quite simple, even if making it happen can be time-consuming and difficult. Only send your newsletter to people who are likely to enjoy whatever book you're telling them about. This means that you don't want everyone on the planet reading your newsletter. Newsletters (and the lists of readers those newsletters are sent to) provide an invaluable resource for each new book you release. No advertising in existence beats telling people who are interested in a product that such a product is available and telling them where they can get one of their very own.

The reasons you want to restrict the readers on your list only to those who would be interested in what you have to sell them is because this allows you to evaluate the success or failure of any announcement. Plus, it gives you a loyal band of followers who provide information you simply can't get anywhere else. Thinking of ending your series at book 10? Let your newsletter readers know and see what kind of reaction you get. Thinking of writing a new series that might interest these readers? Drop a line about your new possible project and see what the response is.

Reader Magnets

The Catch-22 of newsletters is that getting people to sign up for one works best after those people are already fans of your writing. So how do you start out? For writing nonfiction, it's pretty easy. Make snippets of information available related to your subject with the promise of more complete and detailed information available in newsletter form. Then when your nonfiction book is released, you already have a following of people who are naturally interested in your book. But what about fiction? How do you attract readers before you have any readers?

In simple terms, you have to have already written something. I know some writers who have done this by releasing short stories set in their series world. Same characters. Same genre. Attractive to the same type of readers who would enjoy their novel. At the end of each short story, you put in a link that takes readers to a page where they can sign up for your newsletter. As an alternative, you can publish your first novel and put a link in the back of it. Granted, this doesn't help you sell your first novel, but it does start the email list building process that should benefit later books in the series. Many writers offer their readers something for free if they sign up for their newsletter, but when you're just starting out, be wary of giving away everything you've written to date. If your novel is good enough, your readers will want to know when the next novel in the series is being released. If your novel isn't good enough, you've already lost the battle, so offering trinkets in exchange for their email addresses doesn't provide you with much.

The great thing about reader magnets is that they work whether your novels are self-published or published by the big boys. Note that your giveaway freebees (if you use them) will of necessity be something you create and have total control over.

One important consideration with any giveaway that requires readers to sign up for your newsletter (reader magnets) is that you're attracting exactly the wrong sort of crowd. What I mean by that is: You're attracting people who are looking for something free to read. Later, you try to sell them books. See the conflict? On the other hand, if you put a link in the back of the first novel in your series that allows readers to join the newsletter, you've guaranteed that those readers made it to the back of your book before they signed up. Generally this means they read your book. If they sign up at that point, it means they like what you've written and are interested in the next installment. You'll sign up a lot less total people this way, but the readers you have will be more likely to buy than a bunch of freebie hunters.

Quality leads on your newsletter list are much more valuable than people who will delete your emails without ever opening them.

What about a Blog?

Some authors write more in their blogs than they do their books. For nonfiction authors, blogs can be an effective marketing tool. For fiction writers, blogs provide uncertain benefits at best. It's not hard to imagine a group of readers who love a writer's blog but don't care much for his fiction; yet, they still buy his books out of loyalty. It may seem like any reader is a good reader to have, but in our modern world, this is definitely not true.

Blogs work best for fiction writers when a nonfiction subject overlaps nicely with fiction interests. For example, many hard science-fiction authors are interested in space exploration. If you're a sf author who blogs about the latest space missions and rocket technology being developed, chances are good that a significant block of your readers would be interested in your latest space opera novel. If you're a romance writer who blogs about ways to improve your marital relationship, chances are good many of your blog readers are the same readers buying your novels.

Two main problems keep blogs from being an effective marketing tool when you're first starting out: 1) Time spent getting people to follow your blog could be spent getting people to buy your books, and 2) Blogs are a clumsy and inaccurate tool for reaching your fiction readers. A newsletter directed at readers who want to know when your next book is coming out is much more effective and much less time consuming. Just as with social media such as Twitter and Pinterest, if you're already writing a blog, keep writing it. If you're not writing one yet, there are probably better ways to spend your marketing time.

The World's Oldest Profession

According to Wikipedia, Rudyard Kipling is widely credited with associating the world's oldest profession with prostitution. But Kipling had it wrong. Before any money, goods, or services ever changed hands, somebody had to sell somebody else on the idea of giving up something they wanted for something they wanted more. I would argue then that sales is the world's oldest profession. For writer's, we're selling our books, which often feels like we're selling a piece of ourselves. While we can do that by marching down the street, banging a drum, and yelling, "Buy my books!" it isn't a particularly effective use of our time.

A better way to sell our wares is by using the same method nearly everyone else does: advertising. Notice that I didn't say "a profitable way." While many writers make advertising a cash-in activity, there are no guarantees. Like everything associated with writing, the more skilled you are, the more likely you are to succeed.

Nail the Freebies

The most effective (and most important) forms of advertising writers have available are the ones we don't pay any extra for after the book is published. Get these wrong and you'll end up flushing your entire bank account down the advertising toilet with only a handful of sales to show for it. Get the freebies right and any money you spend on advertising will go further and get better results.

The four free areas that you absolutely, positively must make as good as you can are:

- Cover
- Title
- Tagline
- Blurb

These areas are so important to the success of your book that I've covered each of them individually.

Cover

If your cover doesn't hook your readers, everything else you might do to market the book pales in comparison. All readers judge books by their covers first, even if they don't realize it. In today's information-overdriven world, covers that don't get noticed don't get seen. But getting seen isn't enough. If you manage to attract a reader's eye, you need to convince that eye to linger long enough for its owner to consider your book. So much goes into this nearly instantaneous judgment that no one understands exactly what differentiates a successful cover from one that's merely passable, but there are some criteria we can aim for, some of which are more black and white than others:

- Your cover needs to look great both as a full-size image and as a thumbnail.
- The book's title should be easily readable on the thumbnail image.

- The overall look, color, and font on the cover should match currently-selling novels in your book's genre.
- Put some extra space between the letters of your name and between the letters in the title, meaning each letter is further apart than normal text in a book, like this for example.
- Try to make the cover as pleasing to the eye as possible, meaning it's both pleasant and interesting to look at.
- Keep it simple. In general, simpler covers outsell more complex covers and they're a heck of a lot less work.
- The cover should "pop," meaning it has significant contrast between some of the elements.

What you can't allow is a misrepresentation of your novel. They say you catch more flies with honey than with vinegar. As a writer selling books, your honey is a cover that attracts readers who are most likely to want to buy what you're selling. Your vinegar is a cover that your desired readers don't associate with books they like to read. If you create a great cover that makes your novel look like it's a horror novel, you're not going to attract the science fiction readers you actually wanted. Worse yet, if those horror readers happen to buy your novel and read it, they're probably not going to like it. If this happens, the entire sales funnel collapses around your ears.

Make sure your cover matches your genre.

Most self-published authors buy their covers from professional artists. But not all professional artists are good at designing covers. Not all good cover designers are good at all genres. You, as the writer and publisher, are fully responsible for making sure you get an excellent cover for your novel. Do the research yourself. Insist on changes if needed until you get the cover right.

Title

While titles don't have the same importance as covers or even blurbs and taglines, they should still attract the right kind of reader. The best titles perform triple duty: They're interesting, they convey the genre perfectly, and they catch one or more common search keywords while still being unique. For example, police procedural mysteries might have titles like: *Dead Stop, Her Last Goodbye,* or *The Deepest Grave.* Regency romances might have titles like: *Loving a Noble Gentleman, Amelia and the Viscount,* or *A Governess for the Brooding Duke.*

While some writers will put more emphasis on titles than is necessary, your title is how most word-of-mouth recommendations happen, at least until you become famous. That means you want your book's title to be relatively easy to remember. You also want your series titles to be relatively easy to remember. While titles can't be copyrighted, it's still best to google your title and make sure your book won't get confused with someone else's.

From a practical standpoint, the length of the title comes into play, especially in today's world of shopping via thumbnail. The longer your title, the harder it is to fit on the cover at a size large enough to be readable. Along that line of thinking, don't hesitate to allow small words to be unreadable in the thumbnail. For example, *A Governess for the Brooding Duke* would have the words "for the" in a smaller size that would never be readable in thumbnail form.

Tagline

Strictly speaking, your novel doesn't absolutely need a tagline, but it sure comes in handy. Taglines are simply the shortest way for you to tell a reader just enough about your book to convince them they want to know more. Typically taglines are one sentence long. If each sentence is just a few words, multiple sentences work. For example, the horror movie Willard was based on a novel called *Ratman's Notebooks*. If we were to write a tagline for that novel, we might say:

> A lonely boy. A pack of rats. Sweet revenge.

I'm not saying it's great (Stephen Gilbert's estate isn't paying me to write taglines for his old novel), but it conveys the point. It's horrifying for most people. A boy. Rats. Revenge? It certainly doesn't sound pleasant, which is exactly what we're looking for. This is a dark novel and the tagline should attract readers who are interested in that type of story.

The point of taglines is that potential readers aren't going to give you much of their time unless you do something to give them pause. While it's true that they'll barely glance at your cover, the human eye's incredibly adept at processing visual images into complex information. Readers get a ton out of that glance. When it comes to reading, information trickles in comparison. The problem is that we never know how long a reader will grace us with their attention. A tagline's an attempt to buy yourself a little more of their precious time.

A further benefit of taglines is that they can be reused for paid advertising or even to describe your novel in an elevator pitch. A great tagline never goes to waste.

Blurb

In our self-publishing world, most of us can think of blurbs as Amazon descriptions. Along with your tagline (if you chose to have one), this is what finally convinces that reader to click the "Buy now with 1-Click" or "Add to Cart" button. Once a reader reaches your description, they're interested. They've seen your cover, they've probably read your title, they've seen your tagline, and now they're thinking about making a purchase.

In fairness, part of the success of your blurb depends on how good the book is you've written. It's hard to sell a mediocre book with a great blurb, but that's a lot easier than selling a mediocre book with a mediocre blurb.

A critical consideration is that you only get to tell the reader what appears "above the fold" before they make a decision. The problem with that is that you have no way to know what appears above the fold. Different amounts of text will be visible depending on the screen size. This means that you need to hook the reader as quickly as you can. (See "Tagline" above.) Even if you don't use a tagline, you must always remember that your time with your potential book buyer is limited. Before you convince them to buy, you need to persuade them to click "Read more" and close the sale with what you have below the fold.

The job of your blurb is simple: Convince any potential reader that this is a book that they would like to read, provided they're a reader who really would like to read it. While sales of any kind are nice in the short-term, devoted readers who actually like what you've written are much more important to long-term success. This will become clearer as we go through advertising options, but it's not hard to understand that if more people read all your books instead of just your first book, selling that first book becomes much more valuable.

This is where research comes into play. Every genre is different. You want to appeal to people who will like the type of book you've written. If you followed the advice in the How to Choose" section, this is relatively easy. Remember those tropes you identified? For the blurb, you hit the parts of your story that fulfill those tropes. If you didn't write to market to start, you'll need to reverse-engineer the process. Figure out what books your book resembles and then identify what people were looking for when they bought those books. Put another way, figure out what people are looking for after they read those other books.

Many successful self-published authors claim you also need a call-to-action at the end of your description. This is clearly not the case. While good copywriting dictates you should always have a clear call-to-action, my research indicates that any call-to-action is too strong for most fiction readers. Plus, it's just not necessary. If you're a potential reader looking at a book on Amazon, you don't need to be told what your call-to-action is. Plus, digital calls-to-action are invariably links or buttons you can click. Neither are allowed in an Amazon description. As a result, putting a call-to-action in your Amazon description makes you sound a lot like that author walking down the street and screaming, "Buy my books!"

For non-fiction books, a call-to-action makes a little more sense. In those cases, the call to action is typically subtle, such as "Let's get moving!" or "Don't leave your success up to chance. Do <whatever the book's about> now."

Sometimes Math Is Necessary

Before you spend any money on advertising, you need to know what kind of return you want on your investment. Otherwise you're just throwing money in the air and hoping some eventually drifts back to you.

Even if you're just starting out and you're looking to build a following more than you're looking for positive cash flow, you should still set a pain threshold. For most of your career, you will be looking for a positive cash flow. If you spend $100 on ads and sell books worth $80 in royalties, you just lost $20. Granted, you **might** have gained some readers who **might** buy future books. How do you know? If you have a series of books, you need to calculate your cumulative read-through. That is, how many people who buy the first book in your series buy all the books in your series? While it focuses on Facebook ads, Michael Cooper's *Help! My Facebook Ads Suck* goes into gory detail about how to calculate all this return on investment (and includes a spreadsheet to do the math for you).

The point for our discussion is that you need to know how much a sale is worth. If you have a single e-book in Kindle Unlimited that sells for $10, you get $7 every time you sell a copy of that book. If you spend $5 on advertising for every copy you sell, you make $2 per book. While I don't want to get too far into the math, if you have a series of five books, all of which sell for $3 each, you'd make $10 in royalties if you sold all five books. If you know half the people who buy the first book go on to buy and read all five books and the other half only buy the first one, you'd sell five books for one customer and one book for another. That averages out to three total sales for every person who buys your first book.

Again, don't worry about the math right now if it bothers you. For our very simplified case, we'd know that we sell three total books on average every time we sell that first book in our series. That means $6 in royalties. If we sink $7 in ads to get a sale, it's not worth it. We'd go broke. If we sink $5 in ads to get a sale, we're making a small amount of money with quite a bit of risk.

While all of my examples above relate to online advertising for Kindle Unlimited titles, you can apply the same to any form of advertising. If you spend $30 to print up a thousand handouts and give them to people who pass you on the street corner, then get five sales over the course of the next week, you can calculate whether those flyers were a good investment. Each of those sales cost you $6. Plus a significant amount of your time.

The point is that you need to know how much you spend versus how much you make back. This allows you to try different types of advertising as well as different types of ads and compare the results. Without these calculations, you're just guessing.

One final note: If you don't want to do all this math, just create a single Amazon ad when your book is released. Put in a bid of $0.20 or less per click or lower. You can also set a daily spending limit on Amazon, but chances are you'll never reach it. After a month, you might have only spent $20 or $30. If you've sold a hundred copies of your book during that time (because you're doing everything else you can to market your book), assume the ad is working and let it go.

You can spend half your working day analyzing and tweaking the various forms of advertising you're using to sell your books. Or you could write another couple novels with all those hours. We all have different levels of interest in marketing. If it's something you enjoy, get into it as far as you want. If you hate the very idea, learn enough so that you don't cost yourself a small fortune if you make a mistake.

Pay to Play

The only paid advertising I'll examine from this point on is on-line advertising. While it's perfectly feasible to advertise using billboards, newspapers and magazines, book video trailers, radio and television commercials, and direct mail flyers, the price point for effective entry into any of those advertising mediums is a couple of orders of magnitude higher than it is with on-line advertising. As such, it's much riskier. Most authors who aren't independently wealthy therefore avoid laying out that kind of cash with no promise of return.

As for the on-line advertising market, we'll restrict our discussion to the big three. I call these the "big three" because these are the paid advertising mediums that I know have worked (and worked wildly) for many authors:

- Amazon Ads
- Facebook Ads
- BookBub Promotions

I've covered each of these mediums in the sections below.

Amazon Ads

The single greatest advantage of buying ads through Amazon is that those ads go straight to people who buy books at Amazon. More important, those ads go to people precisely when they're shopping for books on Amazon. This is gold. It's like the impulse items next to the checkout in a grocery store. Your potential readers are buying books. Hey, here's your book! Why not buy it?

While this is pretty wonderful stuff, it's not as good as organically having Amazon freely recommend your books to those same people—a potential sales channel you'll learn about in the next chapter—but it's hard to overestimate the advantage provided by marketing your novel to an audience that's likely to be interested in buying and is already on the site (or in the app) that allows them to make the purchase immediately.

Amazon ads work.

That is, they work if you've done a great job on your cover, title, tagline, and blurb—and you've written a decent book. Also, you need to select a good set of keywords for your Sponsored Products ads and the correct Targeted Interests for your Product Display Ads. There are plenty of specialized books available that will cover exactly how to do Amazon Ads, such as *Mastering Amazon Ads* by Brian D. Meeks.

Amazon ads aren't perfect. There's no guarantee they'll actually make you any money, especially if you're trying to sell a single book rather than a series. Also, Amazon customers are getting fairly jaded against the ads. Many Amazon customers have trained themselves to look at the Also-Boughts but ignore the Sponsored Products. You can get around this by using Product Display Ads by Interest. Those type of ads are sometimes displayed as a person's Kindle screensaver, which means they have sole possession of a reader's interest, however briefly. Also, Amazon ads tend to die after a time. They simply quit working.

For me, this highlights the biggest problem with Amazon ads, which is also a problem with Facebook ads. To work best, they require constant maintenance. Granted, I know authors who start up a single Amazon ad and have it run effectively for months without ever touching it. I know many others who try ten different ads and only get one to work.

The biggest caution I will give is that the effectiveness of Amazon ads changes constantly. Do a bit of research before starting your own sets of Amazon ads.

As far as judging the results of your Amazon ads, here are some handy targets you should be trying to hit:

- Average Cost Per Click (ACPC) should be less than 20¢
- Clicks Per 1,000 Impressions should be 1 or higher
- Average Clicks Per Sale should be between 5 and 20 with a reasonable goal of 10

If you hit the ACPS goal, you're going to spend $1.50-$2.00 for every book you sell. Certainly I know a lot of writers who do much better than this with their ads, but most of them devote a lot of time to tweaking, creating, and maintaining those ads. Even so, if you have multiple books in your series, advertise the first one only (except the first few weeks after each release of a new book in the series) and it won't take long for you to be making real money if you can maintain sales from this amount of advertising.

Getting a click every 1,000 impressions tells you if your ad is working. Plus, Amazon tends to limit ads (not show them much) for any ads that get less than one click per 1,000 impressions.

Having those clicks cost less than 20¢ each just means you have a better chance that you'll make a profit on the ads. Also, there doesn't seem to be any relationship between paying more for your ad and getting any additional sales. Why pay more for less?

If your results don't match the targets I provided above, the ones that are off give you a clue as to what you need to change. If your average cost per click is too high, lower the amount of your bids. If your clicks to impressions ratio is too low, improve your ad blurb, possibly your cover thumbnail, and re-examine your keywords. If your average clicks per sale is too high, work on your cover, your tagline, or your description.

This is where being a self-published author blows the sock off most traditional routes to publication. You can tweak your book's marketing after publication. Change the cover? Definitely possible. Improve the blurb? No problem.

One of the benefits of Amazon (and Facebook) ads is that you know whether potential readers have viewed your book listing on Amazon. Granted, sometimes folks will accidentally click where they didn't mean to click, but nearly all of the clicks you see on your ad results represent readers who thought your thumbnail and ad copy were interesting enough that they wanted to find out more. If you're getting a ton of clicks and not selling, either you're attracting the wrong type of readers or your cover/tagline/blurb need improvement.

Facebook Ads

In my experience, Facebook ads are more expensive and result in fewer sales per click. So why use them? Mainly because the folks at Amazon Marketing Services are really slow on the uptake in some ways. They may get there eventually, but right now Amazon provides almost no analytics. As a result, you have almost no data related to any Amazon ad beyond the basics of impressions, clicks, and average cost-per-click. Eventually (usually days later) you get information about any sales you may have made.

In comparison, Facebook gives you so many ways to analyze your ad results, you might need a degree in Advertising to take advantage of all the possibilities. For simple writer folks like me, some of the most useful information beyond the basics are the results based on age and gender as well as time of day. How much of this information you want to look at is up to you, but the point is that you can look at it. Facebook makes it available to you.

In addition, there are millions of ways to configure the audience who sees your Facebook ad. You can target by interest, behavior, age, etc. You can save audiences once you get them just right or you can change the audience for an ad after it's ran a few days or weeks. This is great. It's not as good as Amazon ads that automatically target folks while they're in book-buying mode, but it still gives you a great deal of control.

If you want to learn a ton about Facebook ads from someone who's made them work for years, I'd recommend the book I mentioned earlier (Michael Cooper's *Help! My Facebook Ads Suck*). The details of these advertising possibilities are more than worthy of an entire book. Here we're covering what you need to know, but if you want to know more, there are resources available.

In order to judge the results of your Facebook ads (like we did for our Amazon ads), here are some handy targets you should be trying to hit:

- Average Cost Per Click (ACPC) should be less than 30¢
- Relevancy score of at least 8
- Frequency as close to 1 as you can keep it
- Average Clicks Per Sale should be between 20 and 40 with a reasonable goal of 30

The first thing you should notice about these targets is that they're not nearly as optimistic as the Amazon ad targets. That's because Facebook ads don't work as efficiently as Amazon ads. The people who love Facebook ads might argue, but the simple truth is that it's much harder to sell someone a book when they're not book shopping than it is to sell someone a book when they are book shopping. If everything else is equal, that means it will cost you more per sale using Facebook ads than it will using Amazon ads.

Once again, this begs the question: Why use Facebook ads instead of Amazon ads?

The answer is two-fold: Facebook has millions of users and Facebook will spend your money. The biggest problem advertising on Amazon results from Amazon's limited advertising space. This lack of ad inundation makes the ads that are there more effective, but it means you can give Amazon a daily budget of $10 and Amazon may only spend 50¢ of that. You might be selling a book for every $1 you spend on Amazon, but it takes you two days to sell one book. Some people claim to know how to scale up their advertising on Amazon, but I've seen way more failure stories than success stories for folks who have tried.

If you give Facebook $10 per day to spend, they'll typically spend the whole $10, at least until you've saturated your market. If you're making money on each sale even after deducting your advertising costs, Facebook shines and Amazon comes up short.

Speaking of saturating your market, that brings us to Frequency. That's the number Facebook attaches to your results to let you know how many times each person has seen your ad. Facebook doesn't want to repeat the same ads to the same users, because they discovered folks don't like that. As a result, as your Frequency score climbs, your Relevancy score falls. However, if you have an ad that's working great (has a Relevancy score of 10 with low ACPC and great sales results), there's no harm in letting your Frequency number climb as the ad runs its course. That's why you can ignore the Frequency if you wish and just pay attention to the Relevancy score, which Facebook starts to calculate after 500 impressions or so.

Relevancy is based on multiple factors. In simple terms, if enough people who are shown your ad are interested in your ad, your Relevancy score will be high. If less people are interested, your Relevancy score will be lower. One important note on all of the Facebook ad targets mentioned above: Don't pay attention to any of them until you get at least 500 impressions and obtain that Relevancy score. This is because ads can start off ridiculously high, get a Relevancy score of 10, and perform fantastic afterwards.

Following are some general guidelines about how to construct effective Facebook ads.

People on Facebook aren't shopping, so don't have your ad look like an ad. This means your ad should look more like a normal Facebook post and less like an ad. To do this, use a good picture that does **not** contain text. This means that you should not use the cover of your book. Typically you should also not use part of the cover of your book unless it's a really great picture and doesn't really look like a book cover. This is because Facebook doesn't serve ads that contain text in the picture to nearly as many people while simultaneously charging way more for the people who do respond to the ad. While it's true that Facebook ads with text-containing pictures are allowed as long as they're part of a book cover, but those ads never perform as well as Facebook ads with pictures that don't contain text.

Have all the links in your ad point to your page on Amazon. You typically run Facebook ads to sell your book. Using them for anything else is prohibitively expensive compared to other methods of advertising.

Also consider getting another Amazon account and use it as your Amazon Affiliate account. Then use a different Affiliate tag for each ad. This changes your Click-Through data into sales data. Note that Amazon says this is prohibited. If they discover you're doing it, they'll shut down your Affiliate account, but it's the only current way to track sales results on Amazon from non-Amazon ads until Amazon wises up and provides us with a way to do that.

BookBub Promotions

The original idea behind BookBub was simple. Readers signed up to receive daily emails with great offers on the types of books they like to read. The authors of those books deeply discounted the books in order to get into the Bookbub email. Readers received access to inexpensive (or free) books from authors they probably wouldn't have found any other way and authors received a huge boost to the number of books they get into readers' hands.

This all sounds fairly wonderful. And it was.

BookBub is still good if you can talk BookBub into letting you have a promotion. Unfortunately, for new authors, you need to be relatively successful before BookBub is likely to give you a chance. What do I mean by that? BookBub says they're looking to promote books to their readers that come with tons of existing, positive reader reviews, several positive critical reviews, and awards or celebrity recommendations. In simple terms, BookBub wants to promote your book if they have strong indications that it's a darned good book that tons of people already like and have recommended.

In my experience, if your book gained that much press and positive momentum, you don't need BookBub's help. However, that doesn't mean receiving a BookBub promotion won't greatly increase your income from an already successful book. That's why it's so difficult for new, relatively unknown writers to get a BookBub promotion. As a result, BookBub has way more authors who want to get their books in front of BookBub's rabid readers than BookBub has slots available. As a result, while getting a BookBub deal remains possible, it's not an easy or automatic possibility.

The second problem is that BookBub doesn't do this for free. Bookbub deals are expensive and you need to pay for them in advance. That means you lay out thousands of dollars in hopes you get more than your investment back. From the authors I've talked to, they've nearly always been ecstatic about their BookBub results, but research this potential hand grenade before you jump on it.

The good news is that you don't need to do much to make a BookBub deal work if you're offered one. It's by far the easiest online advertising you can have. Simply be prepared to reduce the price of the book you'd like featured in BookBub's daily email and fill out BookBub's handy-dandy request form. If BookBub agrees to take your book, you need to have your book reduced in price at the proper time and for the proper duration. Amazon's Kindle Unlimited Countdown Deals are a great way to accomplish this. Or you can offer the first book in a multi-book series for free as your BookBub deal. Many readers who like the free book you provide will go on to buy other books in your series.

I've known multiple authors whose careers were jump-started by their BookBub deal.

The problem is that BookBub isn't something you can do whenever you want; it's something you can try to do once in a while. Plus it's a one-shot opportunity for many authors, not part of an ongoing marketing strategy.

Which Way Do I Go?

These three online advertising methods aren't exclusive. Most of the authors I know use all three of them. Readers can be reached in many different ways. If you find an advertising medium that lets you reach readers at a cost less than what you earn in royalties and doesn't suck up your entire life to make it work, it's usually worth the effort.

Feeding the Amazonian Beast

It continues to amaze me when I meet U.S. or British writers who scoff at the importance of Amazon to their writing careers. They talk about other distributors such as Barnes & Noble, Kobo, Apple's iBooks, Google Play, Stanza, and others, as if they matter for a writer starting out. For nearly all new fiction writers, these other distributors literally represent a drop in your revenue stream.

Without question, the largest electronic bookstore in the world is Amazon Kindle. The second largest is Kindle Unlimited. The exact percentage of market share Amazon controls is changing all the time, but if you don't go exclusively with Amazon, you aren't allowed to be part of the Kindle Unlimited program. That means you just set fire to a distribution deal with the second largest bookseller in the world.

There are other reasons to go exclusively with Amazon that go beyond how many novels you can sell:

- One market to target
- One distribution channel to sync
- Higher royalties from Amazon
- Access to an audience you won't reach any other way (readers who only read free books via Kindle Unlimited)
- Ability to run free book promotions and run Kindle Countdown deals and maintain your higher royalties
- Amazon's marketing machine

The first and last items appear similar, but we will see they are not.

Rather than going through these items one by one, I can summarize them quite simply. As of 2017, the easiest way for a new writer to make the most money from their novels is by selling those novels exclusively through Amazon.

Granted, if you have a traditional publishing deal it's unlikely you'll have any say in where your novels are sold—another reason to go the indie route—but even if your novels are distributed through many channels, Amazon still matters a great deal.

Not Just Any Reader

Let's say I give you 100 pears and tell you to sell them in the next two hours. For every pear you sell, you'll get $1. If you sell them all 100, I'll give you a bonus of $1,000. To make your job more interesting, I lead you to a pair of doors. Behind the first door is a group of 1,000 random people I grabbed off the street. Behind the second door I've assembled a group of 200 pear lovers who haven't eaten today and have money in their pockets. After I load you up with the pears, I let you choose which door to go through. How many of you would choose the room with the random group? How many would choose the room filled with pear lovers?

Most writers choose the random group. Why? That group contains more people. Here's the problem: Since they were chosen randomly, we know very little about that group. We can assume some will be hungry, some will like pears, and some will have enough money to buy a pear, but how many will be hungry, like pears, and have money? Probably not enough. Also, each time you try to sell a pear and fail, you won't know why. Maybe they weren't hungry. Maybe they just didn't like the look of your pears. Maybe you shouldn't be trying to sell ice to Eskimos.

For the pear lovers, we know they have the interest and the means to buy your pears. If they don't buy, it's pretty clear the problem isn't with them.

But here's where it gets interesting.

What if I tell you that if you manage to sell half your pears to the pear lovers, I'll immediately bring an additional 500 pear lovers into the room and give you an additional two hours to sell the pears? The more pears you sell, the more hungry pear lovers I'll push into your room and the more time I'll give you.

Now how many of you would choose to sell to the random group?

What if I told you a couple dozen other people were going to be selling all kinds of fruit in each room at the same time you're trying to sell your pears? That room filled with pear lovers is looking pretty good now, isn't it?

This may seem like a silly example, but it's not all that different that what actually happens on Amazon. The difference is that Amazon doesn't decide what kind of people to bring into the room based on what you're selling. Instead, they look at what else the people who are buying your book are also buying and they use that knowledge to select the next group of people (if any) to bring into the room.

No More Pears

Amazon is the DM (data master) of the book buying world. They've spent over 20 years figuring out how to sell books online. What they discovered early is that data is the key to success. The biggest problem faced by every avid reader is finding the next novel they want to read. Amazon knows that recommending the right books to the right readers means they will sell more books. This doesn't make Amazon the big bad. Far from it. It makes readers happier and allows authors to sell more books. Granted, both Amazon (and the authors they recommend) will make a lot more money, but that's why people go into business: to make money. The difficulty for Amazon is identifying books their readers would like to read.

It's no surprise then that readers who have the narrowest focuses are the easiest to please, provided there are enough books they would like available. If the only books a reader buys are military science fiction, you wouldn't recommend they try a historical romance. On the other hand, if a reader intermittently buys romances, mysteries, self-help nonfiction, fantasies, biographies, police procedurals, and mainstream award-winning books, how do you recommend that perfect next novel? You don't know—and neither does Amazon.

Which brings us to your newly released novel. If you sell, for example, 50 copies of that novel, Amazon's data crunching machines examine the buyers who purchased those copies. If 46 are readers who mostly buy military science-fiction novels, Amazon concludes that you must have written a military science-fiction novel. That's when those vast stores of data come in handy. Amazon knows that of those 46 readers, half also bought three other military science-fiction novels. In this simple example, any idiot could readily identify a likely group of readers who might like your novel: It's the set of readers who purchased those other three novels but haven't yet bought yours.

For many reasons, Amazon doesn't immediately hawk your book to this group of readers. Instead they let a select group of those readers know about your new novel. If a significant portion of those readers check out your book and decide to buy it, all those electrons at Amazon start to get excited. The emails and notifications start to fly. More potential readers flock to your book's page on Amazon. If those readers like what they see and keep buying, Amazon rightly decides to ride the wave. Suddenly you go from selling 50 novels to 5,000. The next thing you know, Amazon's mighty marketing machine is driving readers to your page in a way that's impossible to buy or replicate.

What's best about this approach is that everybody wins. Readers discover a new author who they want to read, the writer finds readers who want to buy their book, and Amazon sells more books. As an added bonus, this system is incredibly difficult to game. Even if you went out and created 50 user accounts and had those accounts buy books you thought were similar to yours, the initial, tentative marketing push by Amazon on your behalf would only succeed if readers who checked out your novel actually bought it. On the other hand, if your cover or your summary isn't up to snuff, not enough of those readers would think your novel looked all that interesting. They wouldn't buy the book. Amazon would then halt the marketing push before it really started. Don't forget, not only will those buyers be influenced by your cover and your blurb, they'll also be influenced by the reviews that start streaming in. If half the readers who buy your novel hate it, you aren't going to sell many more copies.

The system only works when everybody wins.

Death by Amazon

At this point, most folks out there start pointing out the obvious flaw in this marketing system. "Ya, but what about when Amazon changes their marketing model?"

I can't say this will never happen. Someday Amazon will almost certainly become too big for its britches. Executives there will make that stupid and greedy decision to take advantage of the authors who've helped them to unprecedented success, but that decision won't come easily.

It's not that Amazon is pure of heart. They're in the business of selling books (among many other things). To do so, they need to keep their readers happy. They might reduce the profit margins for authors. They might favor the books they publish themselves over every other publisher.

Here's what won't change: If you write a great novel that a readily identifiable group of people enjoy reading, Amazon will drive those readers to your page. To do anything else would reduce the number of books they sell for no good reason.

The big traditional publishing houses have already allowed their hubris to drive the best and brightest of the new authors from their ranks. Readers followed. If Amazon repeats those mistakes, another company will step in to fill the void. It's not that the traditional publishing houses were stupid or intentionally harsh. They were maximizing their profits based on the business logic of the day. That business logic changed, and they were slow to adapt, but they're getting there.

A Helping Hand

When it comes to marketing in an Amazon driven world, the best technique you can use to sell your new novel, regardless whether it's traditionally published or indie, is to identify a loyal group of readers who like the type of novel you've written and will want to buy that novel as soon as it's released.

This is the hard part.

Sure, after you have tons of success, this is easy. At that point, readers are seeking you out. But what about when you're first getting started? How do you find those readers then?

The truth is, it can be hard and typically involves a decent amount of effort. The techniques needed for success are a book unto themselves. I talked about Reader Magnets in the Newsletter section, but finding that loyal group of readers, especially for your first novel, involves much more than that. If possible, you need to use every marketing technique I cover here plus a few more I haven't thought of. Or you just need to master one of them exceptionally well. Or you just need to get lucky. No, I'm not confused. It's just that there's no easy one-size-fits-all answer. What works great for one writer may not work for others.

The best single piece of advice I can provide here is to do some prep work before you launch your novel. Try to come up with as many readers as you can however you can. Continue the process immediately after the novel launches. Remember, you want to mainly attract folks who typically buy books on Amazon similar to the one you're selling. The absolute best and most powerful marketing you can get is to have someone else (Amazon in this case) do the marketing for you. The sooner you can get them to take over the job, the better you will do. The easiest way to do that is to sell books right from the start and keep selling books, especially when those books are sold to a group of readers with similar tastes.

There is too much. Let me sum up

Marketing is important to all writers at every stage of their careers. No matter how successful you are, you can increase your success through marketing, if you do it well.

- Similar techniques can be used to market a novel regardless whether it is traditionally or self published.
- The main branding control all authors maintain is the author name they attach to their novels. The easiest way to help your readers distinguish between the different types (genres) of books you write is by using a pseudonym unique to each.
- The most efficient type of marketing an author can do always involves reaching the greatest number of potential readers for each marketing action taken. For example, being interviewed for any public media format is always more effective than doing a book-signing.
- Use as many types of marketing as you can to get the word out to your readers, including doing interviews and press releases, having a web page, sending a newsletter to readers of your previous work, encouraging book reviews, and employing advertising targeted toward likely readers.
- Beware communicating repeatedly through any social medium (such as your personal Twitter account, your personal Facebook page, Pinterest, your blog, etc.) that reaches a general group of

readers rather than a select group likely to buy books similar to the one you're selling.

- The most important marketing you must get right is the information directly attached to your novel: cover, title, tagline, and blurb (description).
- Your cover should look great as a full image and a thumbnail, should pop with at least one area of contrast, have easy-to-read and pleasing fonts, and should have a readable title, even when viewed as a thumbnail.
- Having an interesting tagline gives you more time to convince a potential reader to buy your book.
- The only job your book's blurb/description has is to sell your book without misrepresenting it.
- Amazon ads tend to be the most efficient, common, on-line ads but they're difficult to scale and degrade over time.
- Facebook ads are easier to scale but are less efficient and tend to cost more than Amazon ads per sale
- BookBub promotions are effective and lucrative if you can get them, which is much easier to do with some success already under your belt.
- Selling exclusively through Amazon is currently the most reliable way for a new writer to make money while building a loyal group of readers.
- Not all readers are created equal.
- When you release a novel, do everything in your power to sell that novel to readers who like

books similar to the one you just released. If you're successful, chances are good that Amazon will take over the marketing for you. As a result, you'll sell more books than you could through nearly any other means.

A Final Word

The most important criteria, by far, for becoming a successful self-published author is creating as much great, finished material as you can. If you have ten good books in print, those are infinitely better than one great manuscript waiting to be discovered.

To help you do just that, please consider the other books in the Write a Great Novel series:

- *Writing Quickly While Writing Well*
- *Story and Characters*
- *Beginning to End*

If you'd prefer, you can all the books from the Write a Great Novel series compiled into one handy volume (which will always be less expensive than buying the books individually):

- *Write a Great Novel: The Wonderful Writing Secrets of Oz*

If you have any writing-related questions, don't hesitate to contact me by leaving a comment on my Facebook page: http://www.facebook.com/grsixbury/

Index

www.ingramcontent.com/pod-product-compliance
Lightning Source LLC
Chambersburg PA
CBHW022118280326
41933CB00007B/439